The Essential Craft Cocktail Recipe Book

By Carla Hutson

Table of Contents

Citrus Rosé Sangria Recipe

Are you looking for a new and exciting drink to serve at your next gathering? Citrus Ros Sangria is the perfect solution! This delicious and refreshing cocktail has various fruits, spices, and sweet wines. It's easy to make and always a hit with guests. Whether you're throwing a party or having a few friends over for drinks, this citrus ros sangria recipe will have everyone asking for seconds.

Prep Time 5 minutes Total Time 5 minutes

Ingredients:

- ✓ 1 bottle (750 ml) rosé wine, chilled
- ✓ 1 cup freshly squeezed orange juice
- ✓ 1/4 cup freshly squeezed lemon juice
- ✓ 1/4 cup freshly squeezed lime juice
- ✓ 1/4 cup simple syrup (adjust to taste)
- ✓ 1/2 cup brandy or orange liqueur (e.g., Cointreau, Grand Marnier)
- ✓ 1 orange, thinly sliced
- ✓ 1 lemon, thinly sliced
- ✓ 1 lime, thinly sliced
- ✓ 1 cup fresh strawberries, hulled and halved
- ✓ 1 cup seedless red or green grapes, halved
- ✓ Ice cubes
- ✓ 1 cup club soda or sparkling water, chilled
- ✓ Fresh mint leaves, for garnish (optional)

Instructions

1. Combine liquids: In a large pitcher, combine the chilled rosé wine, orange juice, lemon juice, lime juice, simple syrup, and brandy or orange liqueur. Stir well to mix.
2. Add fruit: Add the orange, lemon, and lime slices, as well as the strawberries and grapes to the pitcher. Gently stir to combine.
3. Chill the sangria: Cover the pitcher and refrigerate for at least 2 hours, or preferably overnight, to allow the flavors to meld together and the fruit to infuse the sangria.

4. Serve: When ready to serve, fill glasses with ice cubes. Pour the sangria mixture into the glasses, including some of the fruit. Top each glass with a chilled club soda or sparkling water splash for some effervescence.

5. Garnish and enjoy: Garnish each glass with fresh mint leaves, if desired. Then, immediately serve the Citrus Rosé Sangria Cocktail and enjoy this refreshing, fruity beverage!

Sparkling Campari Orange

The classic Italian aperitif Campari has long been a staple of the bar scene. But now, the iconic liqueur has been given a sparkling twist with its newest product: Sparkling Campari Orange. This refreshing combination of sweetish Citrus flavored soda and bitter orange-flavored Campari will become an instant favorite amongst cocktail lovers.

Prep Time 4 minutes Total Time 4 minutes

Ingredients:

- ✓ 1.5 oz Campari
- ✓ 2 oz freshly squeezed orange juice
- ✓ 1.5 oz prosecco or other sparkling wine, chilled
- ✓ Ice cubes
- ✓ Orange twist or slice, for garnish
- ✓ Optional: a splash of club soda or sparkling water

Instructions

1. Prepare the glass: Fill a rocks glass or a stemless wine glass with ice cubes.
2. Add Campari and orange juice: Pour the freshly squeezed orange juice over the ice.
3. Top with prosecco: Gently pour the chilled prosecco or sparkling wine into the glass.
4. Optional: Add a splash of club soda or sparkling water if you prefer a lighter, more effervescent cocktail.
5. Stir gently: Use a cocktail spoon or a regular spoon to gently stir the ingredients, careful not to disturb the bubbles from the prosecco.
6. Garnish and serve: Garnish the cocktail with an orange twist or slice. Then, serve immediately and enjoy this refreshing Sparkling Campari Orange Cocktail!

Best Vegas Bomb Recipe

Are you tired of the same old drinks? Want to spice up your next party or gathering? Look no further than the Vegas Bomb, an exciting and delicious cocktail that will bring life to any event. This drink is flavorful and relatively easy to make - all you need are a few essential ingredients. In this recipe, we will share with you the best Vegas Bomb recipe so you can give your guests an unforgettable experience.

Prep Time 7 mins Total Time 7 mins

Ingredients

- ✓ 2.5 ounces cranberry juice
- ✓ 2 ounces Crown Royal whiskey
- ✓ 2 ounces peach schnapps
- ✓ 1.5 ounces Red Bull energy drink
- ✓ Ice optional

Instructions

1. Chill all ingredients.
2. Set out a tall glass tumbler and a shot glass.
3. Measure and pour the cranberry juice, Crown Royal, and peach schnapps into the tumbler. Stir well.
4. Then pour the Red Bull into the shot glass.
5. Serve both glasses and let the partaker drop the shot of Red Bull into their tumbler. (The higher they hold it, the bigger the splash.)

Jameson Old Fashioned

The Jameson Old Fashioned is a classic whiskey cocktail with a hint of sweetness and a little bitterness. This iconic drink has been around since the 1800s, but has become increasingly popular in recent years due to its flavor profile. Whether you're a fan of whiskey drinks or just looking for something new to try, the Jameson Old Fashioned is worth sampling.

PREP TIME 7 minutes TOTAL TIME 7 minutes

Ingredients

- ✓ 5 oz Jameson whiskey
- ✓ 2 tbsp agave nectar
- ✓ 7 dashes of angostura or orange bitters
- ✓ ice
- ✓ 2.5 strips of orange peel

Instructions

1. Combine whiskey, agave and bitters with ice in a cocktail shaker.
2. Shake the cocktail for about 35 seconds.
3. Pour into 2 short cocktail glasses filled with ice. (preferably 1 large ice cube)
4. Twist orange peels and add to glasses.

Easy Pomegranate Margaritas

If you're looking for a delicious and easy cocktail, look no further than the pomegranate margarita! This light and fruity drink is the perfect way to impress your friends at any summer gathering. It's also incredibly simple to make, requiring just a few essential ingredients that can easily be found at your local grocery store. Plus, it has the added benefit of being healthier than other fruity cocktails due to its use of fresh fruit juice.

PREP TIME 15 mins TOTAL TIME 15 mins

Ingredients

- ✓ 2.5 cups pure pomegranate juice
- ✓ 1.5 cups fresh squeezed lime juice
- ✓ 1 cup tequila
- ✓ 1 cup Cointreau or Triple Sec
- ✓ 3.5 cups ice
- ✓ 2/3 cup pomegranate seeds, for garnish
- ✓ Lime wedges, for garnish

Instructions

In a pitcher add the pomegranate juice, lime juice, tequila, and Cointreau (or triple sec) and mix until well combined. Taste and adjust if needed (more juice, more lime, more tequila, etc). Divide among ice filled glasses, and garnish with pomegranate seeds and lime wedges. Serve at once.

Pumpkin Apple Shandy

The start of autumn promises a delicious new beverage - the pumpkin apple shandy. This seasonal drink is a delightful combination of two classic flavors and will satisfy your cravings for something sweet and spicy. In addition, the pumpkin apple shandy can be served hot or cold, depending on preference, making it an ideal beverage for any time of year.

PREP TIME 5 minutes TOTAL TIME 5 minutes

Ingredients:

- ✓ 1.5 oz pumpkin spice liqueur
- ✓ 2 oz apple cider (fresh, if possible)
- ✓ 1/2 oz freshly squeezed lemon juice
- ✓ 6 oz lager or pilsner beer, chilled
- ✓ Ice cubes
- ✓ Cinnamon stick, for garnish (optional)
- ✓ Apple slice, for garnish (optional)

Instructions

1. Combine pumpkin spice liqueur, apple cider, and lemon juice: In a cocktail shaker, combine the pumpkin spice liqueur, apple cider, and freshly squeezed lemon juice.
2. Shake well: Fill the cocktail shaker with ice cubes, secure the lid, and shake the mixture vigorously for about 10-15 seconds to chill and combine the ingredients.
3. Strain into a glass: Fill a pint or tall glass with ice cubes, and strain the shaken mixture over the ice.
4. Top with beer: Slowly pour the chilled lager or pilsner beer into the glass, allowing the mixture to settle before adding more.
5. Gently stir: Use a cocktail spoon or a regular spoon to gently stir the ingredients, careful not to disturb the bubbles from the beer.
6. Garnish and serve: Garnish the Pumpkin Apple Shandy Cocktail with a cinnamon stick and an apple slice, if desired. Serve immediately and enjoy this seasonal, refreshing drink!

Frosting Shots

Summer is here, so it's time to get creative with your cocktails! Frosting Shots are a delicious and easy-to-make dessert cocktail that will take your summer party up a notch. This tasty beverage combines sweet frosting with creamy liqueur for a fun and flavorful spin on classic cocktails. It's the perfect way to cool off in the heat while enjoying an indulgent treat.

Prep Time 5 mins Total Time 5 mins

Ingredients:

- ✓ 1 cup whipped cream vodka
- ✓ 1/2 cup white chocolate liqueur (such as Godiva)
- ✓ 1/2 cup vanilla frosting
- ✓ 1/4 cup milk or heavy cream
- ✓ Ice
- ✓ Colored sugar sprinkles (optional, for rimming the shot glasses)
- ✓ Whipped cream (optional, for topping)

Instructions:

1. Prepare the shot glasses: If you want to add a festive touch, dip the rim of each shot glass in a small amount of vanilla frosting, then roll the rim in colored sugar sprinkles. Set the glasses aside.
2. Combine the whipped cream vodka, white chocolate liqueur, vanilla frosting, and milk or heavy cream in a blender. Blend the mixture until smooth and well combined.
3. Fill a cocktail shaker halfway with ice. Pour the blended mixture into the shaker and secure the lid tightly.
4. Shake the cocktail vigorously for 15-20 seconds, or until the outside of the shaker is cold and frosty.
5. Carefully strain the mixture into the prepared shot glasses, filling them up to the rim.
6. Optionally, top each shot with a dollop of whipped cream and additional sugar sprinkles for a festive touch.

Sloe Gin Fizz Recipe

The Sloe Gin Fizz is a classic cocktail enjoyed for decades. Its subtle sweetness and refreshing flavor are the perfect drink for summer or evening. It combines sloe gin, lemon juice, simple syrup, club soda and an egg white to create a unique blend of flavors. This cocktail is easy to make, requiring just a few ingredients that can be found in most households.

Prep Time 7 mins Total Time 7 mins

Ingredients

- ✓ 3 ounces Sloe Gin
- ✓ 2 tablespoons simple syrup
- ✓ 1 ounce lime juice
- ✓ 1 ounce lemon juice
- ✓ 1.5 cans of club soda

Instructions

1. Combine Sloe Gin, simple syrup, lemon juice and lime juice in a shaker with cracked ice.
2. Shake, pour and top with club soda. Serve.

Kentucky Lemonade

Summertime is the perfect time to try out something new. So if you want to mix up your usual cocktail routine, why not try the Kentucky Lemonade? This delicious, easy-to-make cocktail will become a go-to for your summer gatherings. Packed with flavor and just a hint of sweetness, this twist on the classic lemonade offers refreshing sips you won't forget.

Prep Time 7 mins Cook Time 7 mins Total Time 14 mins

Ingredients

- ✓ 1 cup granulated sugar
- ✓ 1 cup water
- ✓ 2 cups fresh lemon juice (from approximately 6 lemons)
- ✓ 2/3 cup fresh mint leaves
- ✓ 1 cup Bourbon (depending on your tastes)
- ✓ 7 cups ginger ale
- ✓ additional lemon slices (for garnish)

Instructions

1. In a small saucepan, combine granulated sugar and water and heat over MED heat. Heat until sugar dissolves into water and the mixture is clear. Simmer for 3 minutes, then remove from heat.
2. Add lemon juice, mint leaves, and Bourbon, then cool the mixture.
3. Pour mixture through a fine strainer into a large pitcher to remove solid precipes and mint leaves. Add ginger ale and stir to combine. Add ice and lemon slices and serve cold.
4. To serve as pictured: Add some water, lemon juice or light corn syrup to a shallow plate. To another shallow plate, add coarse white sugar. Dip the open end of the glasses onto the liquid plate, then onto the sugar plate to create the sugar rim. Serve drink over ice cubes, garnish with a lemon slice and sprig of mint.

OAXACAN RUSTY NAIL

The Oaxacan Rusty Nail is a unique and flavorful cocktail that combines two classic liqueurs - tequila and Drambuie. Originating from the Mexican state of Oaxaca, this delicious drink has become an increasingly popular choice at bars and restaurants worldwide. The combination of smoky tequila, sweet honey-flavored Drambuie and citrus juice creates a complex flavor profile perfect for sipping on a summer night.

prep time: 3 MINUTES total time: 3 MINUTES

INGREDIENTS

- ✓ 2 ounces mezcal (or tequila)
- ✓ 1 ounce Drambuie
- ✓ 4 dashes orange bitters
- ✓ optional: 1.5 slice jalapeño
- ✓ ice
- ✓ 1.5 orange peel

INSTRUCTIONS

1. Add mezcal, Drambuie, orange bitters, and jalapeño slice (if using) to a cocktail shaker. Use a muddler or a spoon to muddle the jalapeño slightly.
2. Add a handful of ice to the cocktail shaker, and stir or shake vigorously for 25 seconds or until the mixture is completely chilled.
3. Run the orange peel around the rim of the glass. Then twist it to express the oils, and place it in the glass. Strain the chilled cocktail mixture on top of the orange peel.
4. Serve immediately.

PINK CHAMPAGNE SANGRIA

If you're looking for a delicious and sophisticated cocktail to impress your friends with, why not try making a pink champagne sangria? This festive and flavorful beverage is the perfect way to celebrate any special occasion such as a birthday or holiday gathering. Combining dry sparkling wine with fresh fruit juice, liqueur, and sweetener, this easy-to-make drink will surely be a crowd-pleaser. Not only is it visually stunning but its taste is equally exquisite.

PREP TIME: 7 MINUTES TOTAL TIME: 7 MINUTES

INGREDIENTS

- ✓ 2/3 cup water
- ✓ 2/3 cup sugar
- ✓ 2/3 cup fresh mint chopped
- ✓ 2.5 cups ruby red grapefruit juice
- ✓ 1.5 cups Pomegranate juice
- ✓ 1.5 bottles Barefoot Bubbly Pink Moscato
- ✓ sliced grapefruit pomegranate arils, and fresh mint for garnish

INSTRUCTIONS

1. Heat water, sugar, and chopped mint in a small saucepan over medium/high heat. Bring to a boil and then reduce to a simmer, stirring occasionally. Allow to simmer for about 12 minutes. Set aside.
2. In a pitcher, combine the simple mint syrup (made in the saucepan above), both juices, and the full bottle of Bubbly Pink Moscato. Stir to combine.
3. Add great grapefruit slices and pomegranate arils into the pitcher.
4. Chill until ready to serve, at least 2 hours.
5. Enjoy!

Creamsicle Delight

Finding new ways to spruce up traditional drinks is always fun, and the Creamsicle Delight cocktail is no exception! This delicious and creamy beverage is a modern twist on the classic cocktails we all know and love. Not only does this enjoyable drink taste great, but it also looks pretty with its bright orange hue. In addition, this delightful concoction is easy and can be tailored to any taste preference.

Total Time: 7 minutes

Ingredients

- ✓ 2 parts whipped vodka
- ✓ 3 parts orange soda or orange juice
- ✓ 3 parts ginger ale
- ✓ Orange wedges and/or maraschino cherry for garnish (optional)

Instructions

1. Pour vodka, orange soda (or juice) and ginger ale in a glass with ice. Stir to combine.
2. Garnish with an orange wedge and/or maraschino cherry, if desired.

Irish Cream Pie Cocktail

If you're looking for a delicious and unique cocktail to serve at your next gathering, the Irish Cream Pie Cocktail is a perfect choice! This fun twist on a classic favorite combines all the flavors of a traditional Irish cream pie with some delightful ingredients for an exceptional cocktail. With its creamy texture and sweet taste, it will surely be a hit with adults and children.

Total Time 7 min

Ingredients

- ✓ 7 ounces Irish Cream
- ✓ 3 ounces vanilla vodka
- ✓ 5 ounces cold coffee
- ✓ 3 ounces milk
- ✓ Ice if desired
- ✓ Honey or corn syrup for rimming glasses
- ✓ Walkers Shortbread Cookies for dipping and garnish

Instructions

1. Crush one shortbread cookie and place on a shallow plate. Place honey or corn syrup on another shallow plate. Dip each glass upside down in the honey and then in the cookie crumbs to rim.
2. Place Irish Cream, vodka, coffee, and milk in a cocktail shaker with ice. Shake, then strain into glasses. Serve over ice, if desired.
3. Serve with more shortbread cookies for dipping.

Clean blackberry mint prosecco cocktail

Welcome to the perfect summer refreshment! This Clean Blackberry Mint Prosecco Cocktail is a delicious, and simple, drink recipe that will bring out the best in any gathering. With just four ingredients, this cocktail can be prepared in minutes, ensuring all your guests are happy. You'll love how fresh and light the flavors of blackberry and mint are, while the prosecco adds a touch of sparkle and brings everything together.

Prep Time 5 minutes Total Time 5 minutes

Ingredients

- ✓ 6 fresh or frozen blackberries
- ✓ 4 leaves fresh mint
- ✓ 1.5 tsp lime juice
- ✓ 1.5 tsp honey
- ✓ 9 oz Riondo Prosecco

Instructions

1. Either muddle or food process the first four ingredients.
2. Add ice to a short cocktail glass, then pour the blackberry mint mixture over. Add Riondo Prosecco to fill the glass, stir, and serve.
3. For added detail, you can skewer a mint leaf and blackberry and serve perched on the top of the glass. Enjoy!

Empress Gin French 75 Cocktail

Welcome to the world of cocktail making! Today, we will explore a popular cocktail with an intriguing name - the Empress Gin French 75. This delicious concoction has become a favorite among mixologists and cocktail enthusiasts around the world. It is a unique combination of gin, lemon juice, simple syrup, and sparkling wine, creating an unforgettable flavor sensation. Not only does it look impressive in its champagne flute glass, but it will also leave you wanting more after each sip.

Prep Time 7 minutes Total Time 7 minutes

Ingredients

- ✓ 2 ounces Empress 1908 Gin
- ✓ 1-ounce lemon juice
- ✓ 2/3 ounce simple syrup
- ✓ 4 ounces of champagne, prosecco, or sparkling wine
- ✓ champagne grapes for garnish

Instructions

1. Fill a cocktail shaker halfway with ice.
2. Then pour in the Empress gin, simple syrup, and lemon juice and shake until well chilled.
3. Strain into a coupe glass and top with champagne.
4. Garnish with champagne grapes if desired!

Irish Coffee

Irish Coffee Cocktail is a delicious drink that is sure to please any taste bud. It combines coffee, whiskey, sugar, and cream perfectly. Perfect for a cozy night in or an after dinner treat, this sweet yet potent beverage is the ideal way to end your evening. Originating in Ireland in the 1940s, the Irish Coffee Cocktail has become a worldwide favorite among coffee and whiskey connoisseurs.

Prep Time 5 minutes Cook Time 3 minutes Total Time 8 minutes

Ingredients

- ✓ 3/4 cup heavy cream chilled
- ✓ 2 ounces of Irish whiskey
- ✓ 3 teaspoons brown sugar
- ✓ 5 ounces freshly brewed coffee hot

Instructions

1. In a small bowl, add heavy cream and beat until soft peaks form, about 5 minutes.
2. In the bottom of a mug, add whiskey. Add brown sugar and stir to dissolve.
3. Top with hot coffee. Pour the thickened cream over the back of a chilled spoon so it floats on top of the coffee.

Tamarind margarita recipe

Tamarind margarita is a popular cocktail choice for any special occasion or gathering. It combines the sweetness of tamarind with the tangy citrus of lime to create a unique and tasty drink. This recipe is easy to make and can be tailored to anyone's tastes. Whether it's a hot summer day or a chilly winter evening, this refreshing and exotic cocktail will please any crowd.

Total Time 5 mins

Ingredients

- ✓ 3/4 cup Tajin or chili powder , for rimming
- ✓ 2 cups of ice
- ✓ 5 ounces tamarind syrup
- ✓ 2.5 ounces of lime juice
- ✓ 2.5 ounces tequila
- ✓ Lime wedges, for garnish

Instructions

1. Rim a margarita glass with a lime wedge and then rim the Tajin.
2. Add the lime juice, tamarind syrup, and tequila in a blender. Add a cup of ice and blend. Feel free to add more ice if you prefer a thicker margarita.
3. Pour the tamarind margarita into the rimmed margarita glasses.
4. Garnish with a lime wedge.

Raspberry Lemonade Margaritas

When the weather heats up, there's nothing better than a refreshing cocktail to enjoy with friends. Raspberry Lemonade Margaritas are a simple, delicious way to cool off and have fun. Whether you're hosting a party or just unwinding after a long day, these fruity margaritas will make your summer even brighter. Not only do they look beautiful when served in glasses with salted rims, but they also taste amazing!

Total Time 7 mins

Ingredients

For one cocktail:

- ✓ 6.5 ounces raspberry lemonade
- ✓ 2.5 ounces tequila
- ✓ 1.5-ounce triple sec
- ✓ Garnish with raspberries and lemon slices

For a pitcher:

- ✓ 6.5cups raspberry lemonade cold
- ✓ 2.5cups tequila cold
- ✓ 1.5cup triple sec cold
- ✓ Garnish with raspberries and lemon slices

Instructions

1. To make one cocktail: Pour all ingredients over ice, garnish with lemon and raspberry.
2. To make a pitcher: add all ingredients, including lemon slices and raspberries, for garnish. Tip: freeze extra lemonade in ice cube trays, so the drink is not watered and stays cold!

3-Ingredient Peach Lemonade Martini

Are you looking for a delicious and simple cocktail for your next gathering? Look no further than this three-ingredient peach lemonade martini! This easy-to-make drink is the perfect combination of sweet, tart, and bubbly. In only a few minutes, you'll have a refreshing summertime favorite that will please your guests. With just a few ingredients, you can whip up this peach lemonade martini to enjoy with friends on any occasion.

Total Time 4 mins

Ingredients

- ✓ 9 oz lemonade
- ✓ 1.5 oz peach martini mix
- ✓ 2.5 oz Deep Eddy's peach vodka

Instructions

1. Pour the martini mix, lemonade, and vodka into a martini shaker with some ice.
2. Shake until condensation forms on the outside of the martini shaker.
3. Pour into a glass and enjoy!

Frozen Orange Prosecco - Frozecco

If you're looking for an easy and delicious way to cool down during the summer heat, then look no further than the Frozen Orange Prosecco cocktail! This unique cocktail, also known as "Frozecco," is guaranteed to be a favorite of your friends and family. Combining two classic summer flavors - orange juice and prosecco - this recipe requires just 4 simple ingredients and 5 minutes of prep time.

Prep Time 8.10 hours Total Time 8.10 hours

Ingredients

- ✓ 1.5 bottles of sparkling Prosecco
- ✓ 1.5 cups freshly squeezed orange juice
- ✓ 2/3 cup ice cubes
- ✓ 2 tsp sugar optional
- ✓ zest of one orange
- ✓ fresh mint for garnish

Instructions

1. Open the Prosecco and pour it into a 13 x 9-inch baking tray. Place in the freezer overnight.
2. Once ready to make the Frozecco, place the frozen Prosecco into a chunk blender and add the orange juice, ice cubes, sugar and orange zest.
3. Blend on high until the mixture is smooth and looks just like a slushy.
4. Divide the Frozecco between 4 small glasses or two regular-sized jelly wine glasses. You may have to spoon the mixture into the glasses but it'll soften up as it melts.
5. Garnish with a sprig of mint and add a straw. Serve at once.

Mason Jar Margaritas

Summer is here and what better way to enjoy the warm weather than by sipping on a delicious Mason Jar Margarita? This easy-to-make cocktail is the perfect addition to any outdoor gathering and can be customized to create a unique flavor. Not only does it provide a refreshing treat, but it also looks great! With just a few simple ingredients, you'll have an amazing drink that everyone will love.

Prep Time 12 mins Chill Time 4 hrs Total Time 4 hrs 12 mins

Ingredients

- ✓ 65 ounces water
- ✓ 25 ounces frozen limeade (2 cans)
- ✓ 4 tablespoons lime juice optional
- ✓ 25 ounces tequila
- ✓ 25 ounces Paula's Texas Orange or Cointreau

Instructions

1. Mix everything in a large pot.
2. Ladle into 9-ounce mason jars, coming to just below the band area.
3. Place lids and screw on rings, or screw on reusable lids.
4. For ease of transport and storage, put jars back into the original box flat, or onto a large tray.
5. Store in the freezer for at least 4 hours, until ready to serve.
6. Serve margaritas with straws. Margaritas will melt around the outside edges first, but using a straw to break up the mixture will speed the process.

Raspberry Rosé Sangria

Are you looking for the perfect summertime cocktail recipe? If so, look no further than this refreshing and delicious Raspberry Ros Sangria Cocktail. This fruity and flavorful cocktail is a favorite among many and will surely be a hit amongst your family and friends. Combining elements of sangria and lemonade, this one-of-a-kind drink will take your taste buds on a journey of sweet sensations you won't want to miss!

Prep Time: 1 Hour cook Time: 15 Minutes total Time: 1 Hour 15

Ingredients

Raspberry simple syrup (optional):

- ✓ 1.5 cups fresh or frozen raspberries
- ✓ 3 ounces water
- ✓ 3 Tablespoons granulated sugar

Sangria:

- ✓ 2.5cups fresh raspberries
- ✓ 2 lemon thinly sliced
- ✓ 1.5bottle rosé
- ✓ 9 ounces lemon-lime soda or club soda

Instructions

Raspberry simple syrup (optional):

1. In a small saucepan, combine raspberries, water and sugar over medium heat to bring it to a boil.
2. 1.5cup fresh or frozen raspberries,3 ounces water,3 Tablespoons granulated sugar
3. Reduce heat and simmer until the sugar has dissolved and it has thickened to a thin syrup.
4. Turn off heat and let cool for at least 7 minutes.
5. Over a small bowl, push syrup through a mesh sieve to catch all the raspberries seeds, leaving you with only the smooth liquid.

Sangria:

1. In a pitcher, combine simple syrup (optional), raspberries, lemon slices and rosé. Place in fridge to chill for at least 1 hour.
2. 2.5cups fresh raspberries,2 lemon,1.5bottle rosé
3. Add club soda or lemon lime soda to pitcher just before serving and gently stir to combine.
4. 9 ounces lemon-lime soda or club soda
5. Fill each serving glass with ice cubes and fill with sangria. Enjoy!

Basic Michelada Recipe

The Michelada is a classic Mexican cocktail that is perfect for any occasion. It has simple ingredients, yet a complex flavor. The Michelada has been around for centuries, with its origins tracing back to Toluca, Mexico. This recipe will provide a basic Michelada, which can easily be altered or enhanced to suit any taste.

Prep Time 7 minutes Total Time 7 minutes

Ingredients

- ✓ 2.5 ounces of tomato juice
- ✓ 2.5 ounces of your favorite refreshing beer
- ✓ 2/3 lime juice
- ✓ 6 drops tabasco (or to taste)
- ✓ 6 drops Worcestershire (vegan or non-vegan, to taste)
- ✓ 2/3 teaspoon salt
- ✓ 2/3 teaspoon black pepper
- ✓ ice

Instructions

1. On a saucer, mix salt and pepper.
2. Juice half a lime.
3. Use the leftover lime wedge rub it all over the rim of the glass.
4. Dip the rim of the glass in the salt and pepper mixture, ensuring it gets all over the rim.
5. Fill the glass with ice.
6. Add tomato, lime, and a few drops of tabasco and Worcestershire sauce.
7. Top with beer.
8. Add one of the 4 fun garnishes as described above and enjoy.

Spiked Ginger Lemonade

Do you fancy a refreshing summer drink? If so, the spiked ginger lemonade cocktail is the perfect choice! This delicious beverage combines the sweetness of lemonade with a kick of ginger, creating an invigorating and flavorful drink that will tantalize your taste buds. With just a few simple ingredients, you can quickly mix up this classic cocktail for all your special occasions or for simply enjoying on a hot day.

Prep Time 17 mins Total Time 17 mins

Ingredients

- ✓ 1.5 cups sugar
- ✓ 1.5 cups water
- ✓ 7 lemons juiced + 1 lemon for garnish
- ✓ 9 oz vodka
- ✓ 3 oz bottles Bundaberg Ginger Beer

Instructions

1. Combine the sugar and water in a small pot over high heat.
2. Stir continuously until the sugar has dissolved and the liquid boils.
3. Remove from the heat and set aside to cool.
4. Once cooled, add the lemon juice and stir to combine.
5. Fill 4 glasses with ice, pour 3/4 of this mixture into each glass.
6. Add 3 oz of vodka to each glass with 7 oz Bundaberg Ginger Beer.
7. Garnish each glass with a lemon wedge and serve.

Easy Citrus White Wine Sangria

Are you looking for a refreshing and delicious cocktail to serve at your next gathering? Look no further than the Easy Citrus White Wine Sangria Cocktail! This zesty and light drink is perfect for any occasion, from summer barbeques to warm winter gatherings. With its simple ingredients, all your guests can enjoy this delectable sangria.

Prep Time: 15 mins Total Time: 15 mins

Ingredients

- ✓ 1.5 large naval orange, sliced
- ✓ 2.5 lemons, sliced
- ✓ 2.5 limes, sliced
- ✓ 3/4 cup fresh mint leaves
- ✓ 2/3 cup citrus vodka
- ✓ 3 tablespoons agave nectar
- ✓ 3 bottles of dry white wine (i used sauvignon blanc)

Instructions

1. Add all the ingredients to a large pitcher.
2. Stir and serve over ice.
3. Or for BEST results. Cover and let rest in the refrigerator for 4 hours. Then serve over ice!

Homemade Watermelon Infused Vodka

Summer is the perfect time to cool off with a refreshing cocktail. However, choosing what kind of drink to make or buy can be hard with so many options. If you're looking for something unique and delicious, then try making a homemade watermelon-infused vodka cocktail! This recipe is easy to make and sure to impress your friends. Not only does this cocktail have a great taste, but it also adds a beautiful color and flavor to your summer gatherings.

Prep Time 7 minutes Total Time 7 minutes

Ingredients for Watermelon Infused Vodka:

- ✓ 1 small seedless watermelon (or 1/2 of a large one)
- ✓ 1 bottle (750 ml) of vodka (preferably a mid-range brand)

Ingredients for Watermelon Infused Vodka Cocktail:

- ✓ 2 oz watermelon infused vodka
- ✓ 1 oz freshly squeezed lime juice
- ✓ 1/2 oz simple syrup (adjust to taste)
- ✓ Club soda or sparkling water
- ✓ Ice
- ✓ Fresh mint leaves (for garnish)
- ✓ Watermelon wedges (for garnish)

Instructions for Watermelon Infused Vodka:

1. Cut the watermelon into small cubes or chunks, removing the rind.
2. Place the watermelon chunks in a large glass jar or container with a tight-fitting lid.
3. Pour the vodka over the watermelon, making sure all the chunks are submerged. Seal the jar tightly.
4. Store the jar in a cool, dark place for at least 3-5 days, gently shaking the jar once a day to help the flavors meld.

5. After the infusion period, strain the vodka through a fine mesh strainer or cheesecloth, discarding the watermelon chunks. Store the infused vodka in a clean, airtight bottle.

Instructions for Watermelon Infused Vodka Cocktail:

1. Fill a highball or Collins glass with ice.
2. Pour the watermelon infused vodka, lime juice, and simple syrup over the ice.
3. Top up the glass with club soda or sparkling water, leaving about half an inch of space from the rim. Gently stir to combine the ingredients.
4. Garnish with fresh mint leaves and a watermelon wedge.
5. Serve with a straw or a stirrer, and enjoy your refreshing Watermelon Infused Vodka cocktail!

Pineapple Margarita With Sweet And Spicy Rim Salt

Nothing says summer like a refreshing and delicious cocktail, and the Pineapple Margarita With Sweet and Spicy Rim Salt Cocktail is the perfect way to cool off on a hot day. This unique twist on the classic margarita combines sweet pineapple with spicy salt to create an unforgettable flavor. So whether you're hosting a gathering or want to treat yourself, this cocktail will surely be a hit.

Prep time: 15 MINS Cook time: 0 MINS Total time: 15 MINS

Ingredients

- ✓ 2.5 ounces pineapple puree, from ¼ fresh pineapple
- ✓ 2.5 ounces white tequila
- ✓ 1.5 ounce Triple Sec
- ✓ 1.5 ounce fresh lime juice
- ✓ Sweet and Spicy Salt
- ✓ 2 teaspoon sea salt
- ✓ 2 teaspoon sugar
- ✓ 2/3 teaspoon cayenne

Instructions

1. Cut off the top and bottom of a pineapple and then cut it into 4 equal pieces. Use one piece then save the rest for another use. Slice off the peel and the hard inner core, chop the pineapple, and then put it into your blender. Blend on high until smooth. (Note: if you don't have a high-powered blender, you may want to strain the puree so there are no hard bits in it.)
2. Mix the Sweet and Spicy Salt ingredients together in a small dish. Run a cut lime around the rim of a glass then dip the rim into the salt. Fill the glass with ice.
3. 1 teaspoon sea salt,2 teaspoon sugar,2/3 teaspoon cayenne
4. Put a handful of ice into a cocktail mixer or glass jar, add 2 ounces of the pineapple puree, the tequila, triple sec, and lime juice and stir until cold.

5. 2.5ounces pineapple puree,2.5 ounces white tequila,1.5 ounce fresh lime juice,1 ounce Triple Sec
6. Strain the pineapple margarita into the glass and garnish with a slice of pineapple.

Lavender Mojitos

Lavender mojitos are a refreshing twist on the classic summer cocktail. Sweet and slightly floral, these delightful drinks bring a unique flavor to any occasion. Not only are they a great way to cool off during hot summer days, but they are also surprisingly easy to make. You can create the perfect lavender mojito in minutes with just a few ingredients and the right technique.

Prep Time 10 minutes Total Time 10 minutes

Ingredients

- ✓ 11 small mint leaves plus a sprig for garnish
- ✓ 1 oz freshly squeezed lime juice
- ✓ Pinch extrafine sugar
- ✓ 1.5 oz white rum
- ✓ DRY Sparkling Lavender

Instructions

1. Place the mint leaves, lime juice and sugar in the bottom of a heavy-bottomed Collins glass. Gently muddle the mint to release the essential oils, but do not crush or shred the leaves. Stop when you smell the mint.
2. Add the rum and fill the glass with ice. Top with Lavender Dry. Stir.
3. Garnish with a sprig of mint.

Skinny and Seasoned Salty Dog

When it comes to summertime drinks, the Salty Dog is a classic. This refreshing beverage combines salty and sweet flavors that make for an ideal warm-weather cocktail. But if you're looking for a lighter version of this beloved drink, the Skinny and Seasoned Salty Dog is the perfect solution. With fewer calories and more flavor, this cocktail is sure to be a hit at your next barbecue or weekend get-together. Best of all, it's incredibly easy to make.

Prep Time 15 minutes Total Time 15 minutes

Ingredients

For the rim:

- ✓ 5 teaspoons Lawry's Seasoned Salt
- ✓ 2 teaspoon lemon pepper
- ✓ Pinch sugar

For the cocktail:

- ✓ Ice cubes
- ✓ 3/4 grapefruit cut into chunks
- ✓ 2/3 lemon cut into chunks
- ✓ 3/4 cup grapefruit-infused vodka
- ✓ 1 cup lemon-flavored seltzer water

Instructions

1. Combine ingredients for the rim in a shallow dish. Run a lemon wedge around the tips of two rocks or cocktail glasses and dip the rims in the salt mixture.
2. Fill glasses with ice cubes and fruit chunks. Divide vodka and seltzer water evenly between glasses and stir with a spoon.

Tequila Mule

Tequila Mule is a unique and refreshing cocktail that has become increasingly popular recently. Combining simple ingredients, Tequila Mule perfectly balances sweet and spicy flavors. It is easy to make, and even the most discerning drinker can enjoy its unique taste. So whether you're entertaining friends or relaxing alone, Tequila Mule offers something special for everyone.

Prep time: 7 mins Total time: 7 mins

Ingredients:

- ✓ 2 oz tequila
- ✓ 1/2 oz freshly squeezed lime juice
- ✓ 3-4 oz ginger beer
- ✓ Ice
- ✓ Lime wheel or wedge (for garnish)
- ✓ Fresh mint sprig (optional, for garnish)
- ✓ Jalapeño slice (optional, for a spicy twist)

Instructions:

1. Fill a copper mule mug or rocks glass with ice.
2. Pour the tequila and lime juice over the ice.
3. Top up the glass with ginger beer, leaving about half an inch of space from the rim. Gently stir to combine the ingredients.
4. Garnish with a lime wheel or wedge, and a fresh mint sprig if desired. For a spicy twist, add a jalapeño slice as well.
5. Serve with a straw or a stirrer, and enjoy your refreshing Tequila Mule cocktail!

Triple Citrus Margarita

Welcome to the ultimate citrus lover's paradise! This recipe is all about creating a refreshing and delicious triple citrus margarita that will tantalize your taste buds. Whether you're looking for a drink to entertain guests or just wanting to relax with an easy-to-make cocktail, this recipe is sure to hit the spot.

Total Time: 7 mins

Ingredients:

- ✓ 2 oz tequila (preferably silver or blanco)
- ✓ 1 oz triple sec (Cointreau or Grand Marnier for a high-quality option)
- ✓ 1 oz freshly squeezed lime juice
- ✓ 1 oz freshly squeezed orange juice
- ✓ 1 oz freshly squeezed grapefruit juice
- ✓ 1/2 oz simple syrup
- ✓ Ice
- ✓ Salt (for rimming the glass)
- ✓ Lime, orange, and grapefruit wedges (for garnish)

Instructions:

1. Prepare the glass: Moisten the rim of a rock or margarita glass with a lime wedge. Pour some salt onto a small plate and dip the rim of the glass into the salt, ensuring an even coating. Set the glass aside.
2. Combine the tequila, triple sec, lime juice, orange juice, grapefruit juice, and syrup in a cocktail shaker.
3. Fill the shaker halfway with ice and secure the lid tightly. Shake the cocktail vigorously for 15-20 seconds, or until the outside of the shaker is cold and frosty.
4. Fill the prepared glass with fresh ice. Strain the shaken cocktail into the glass.
5. Garnish with lime, orange, and grapefruit wedges, either on the rim of the glass or floated on top of the cocktail.

Made in the USA
Las Vegas, NV
15 December 2024

14359758R00022